ANCIENT INDIA FOR KIDS

Early Civilization and History

Ancient History for Kids
6th Grade Social Studies

BABY PROFESSOR
EDUCATION KIDS

Speedy Publishing LLC

40 E. Main St. #1156

Newark, DE 19711

www.speedypublishing.com

Copyright 2018

In this book, we're going to talk about the history of ancient India. So, let's get right to it!

NILE RIVER

The four earliest human civilizations arose around rivers. The Egyptian civilization began along the Nile River and the Chinese civilization sprang up near the Yellow River. The Tigris River and the Euphrates River gave birth to the ancient civilization of Iraq.

INDUS RIVER

I n the region of South Asia, civilization started along the banks of the Indus River. This civilization was the beginning of ancient India.

EARLY HISTORY OF THE INDUS VALLEY

Archaeologists have discovered the remains of human skeletons in South Asia that can be dated back 75,000 years. At the beginning, these humans lived a nomadic lifestyle, which simply means that they traveled from place to place as they hunted and collected food. Artifacts that have been found show that farming was started there circa 5000 BCE.

Just as with other ancient civilizations, the advent of agriculture meant that human beings could grow their own food and stay in one place as long as there was adequate water and fertile soil.

Cities Grow Into Civilizations

Slowly, step-by-step, these farms began to evolve into cities. The civilization that was started in the proximity of the Indus Valley has been called many different names.

Historians describe it as ancient India or as the Indus Valley civilization. Another common name is the Harappan civilization.

There was an ancient city by the name of Harappa, although there were more than 1,000 cities in the valley. There's evidence that civilization began there circa 3000 BCE. In fact, people from the Indus Valley were more than likely trading with other cultures from Mesopotamia as early as 3200 BCE. Because of this, historians believe that the people of ancient India depended on trade more than the other three early civilizations.

MOUNDS AT HARAPPA

INDUS SCRIPTS

The Mysterious Indus Script

It's believed that the civilization of ancient India was the largest of the first four civilizations. The remains of cities that have been found there could easily have provided homes and work for populations of 80,000 or more. However, it has been very difficult to obtain in-depth information about the people who lived there.

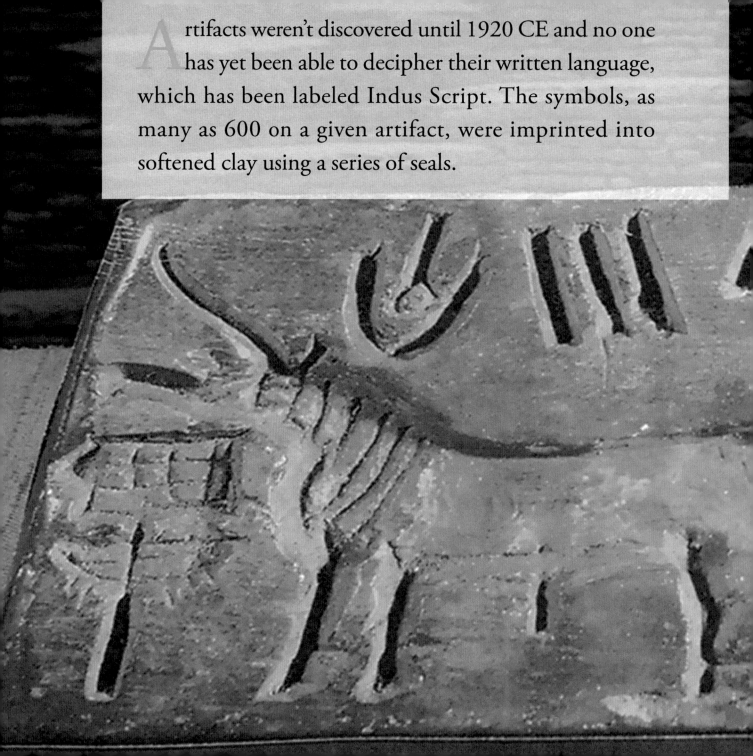

Artifacts weren't discovered until 1920 CE and no one has yet been able to decipher their written language, which has been labeled Indus Script. The symbols, as many as 600 on a given artifact, were imprinted into softened clay using a series of seals.

INDUS CIVILIZATION SEAL
AT INDIAN MUSEUM

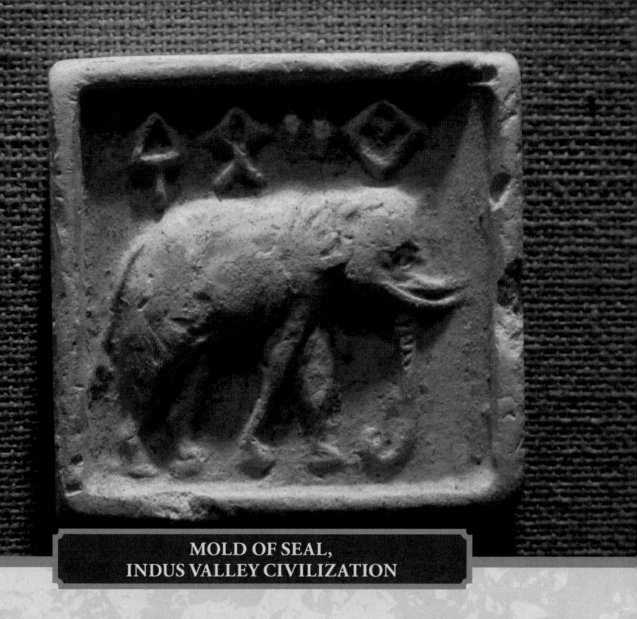

**MOLD OF SEAL,
INDUS VALLEY CIVILIZATION**

Sometimes these seals were created on a cylinder so they could be rolled onto the clay in the same way you would use a rolling pin.

MESOPOTAMIAN CYLINDER SEAL

Symbols from Indus Script have also been found in Mesopotamia. A few of the symbols are similar to the icons of modern-day Hinduism, although historians disagree about their meaning.

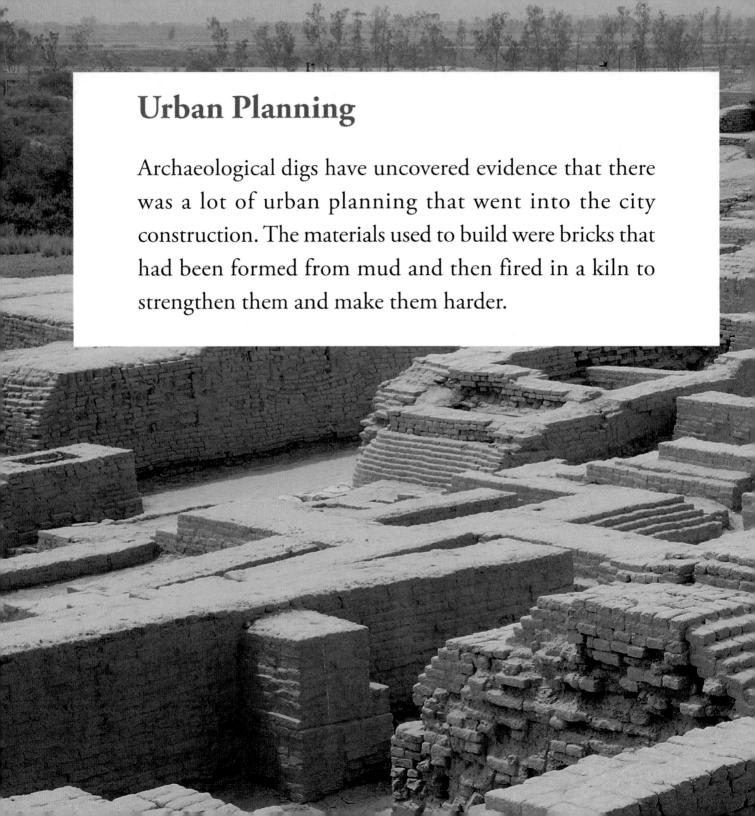

Urban Planning

Archaeological digs have uncovered evidence that there was a lot of urban planning that went into the city construction. The materials used to build were bricks that had been formed from mud and then fired in a kiln to strengthen them and make them harder.

A LARGE WELL AND BATHING
PLATFORMS FROM HARAPPA
OCCUPATION AROUND 2200–1900 BC.

There were sophisticated water wells and systems for water drainage. Most of the city homes had a way to drain water out. At the time, this technology was very advanced and wouldn't be matched in other civilizations

for another 3,000 years. Main roads and side roads were arranged in a grid-like fashion so that there was easy access to the homes.

Farming Was Important

Even with the comfort that these mud-brick homes provided, most people still lived in the farming areas. This was out of necessity since this was still the way that most people ensured that they had enough to feed their families.

MOHENJO DARO, ONE OF THE LARGEST SETTLEMENTS
IN THE ANCIENT INDUS CIVILIZATION

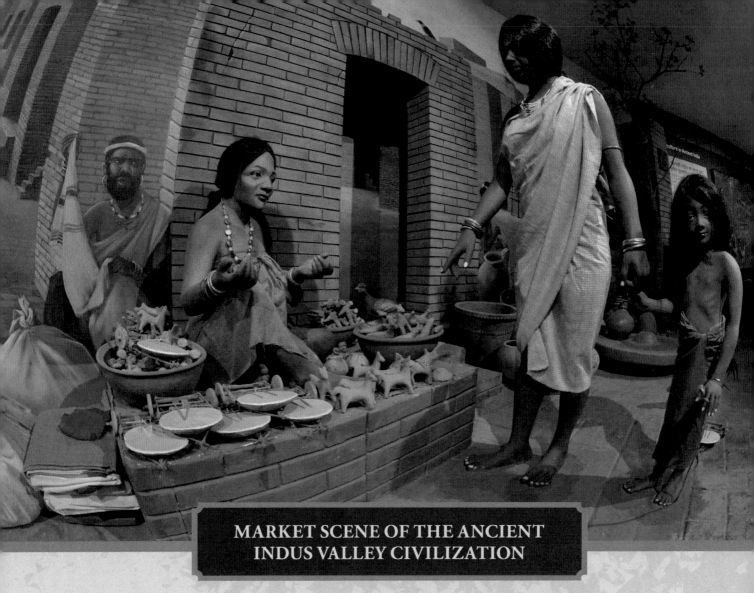

MARKET SCENE OF THE ANCIENT INDUS VALLEY CIVILIZATION

Archaeologists have found that the people of the Indus Valley grew wheat, dates, melons, cotton and sesame seeds. They had also domesticated many types of animals for livestock.

A huge building over 200 feet in length has been uncovered there and some archaeologists believe that it may have been a granary for drying and storing wheat. However, since no remains of grains have been discovered there, the purpose of the building is shrouded in mystery.

VIEW OF GRANARY AND GREAT HALL

An Early Egalitarian Culture

Unlike the people of the civilizations of Egypt and Mesopotamia, the people of the Indus Valley didn't create enormous structures. No large temples or grand palaces have been found.

A PORTION OF THE ANCIENT CITY OF MOHENJO DARO, IN PAKISTAN'S SINDH PROVINCE.

EXCAVATED RUINS OF MOHENJO DARO,
WITH THE GREAT BATH IN THE FOREGROUND

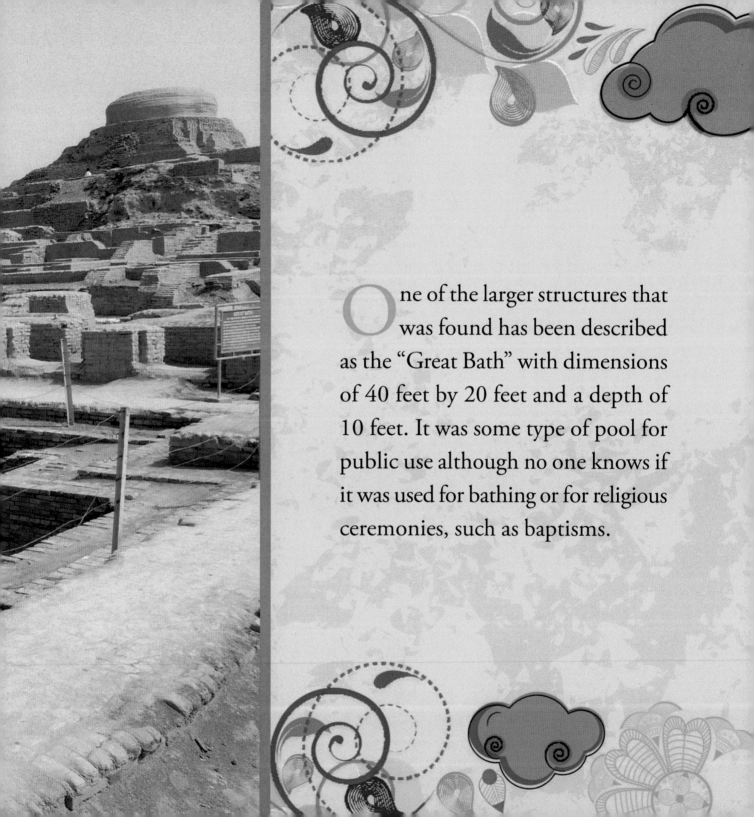

One of the larger structures that was found has been described as the "Great Bath" with dimensions of 40 feet by 20 feet and a depth of 10 feet. It was some type of pool for public use although no one knows if it was used for bathing or for religious ceremonies, such as baptisms.

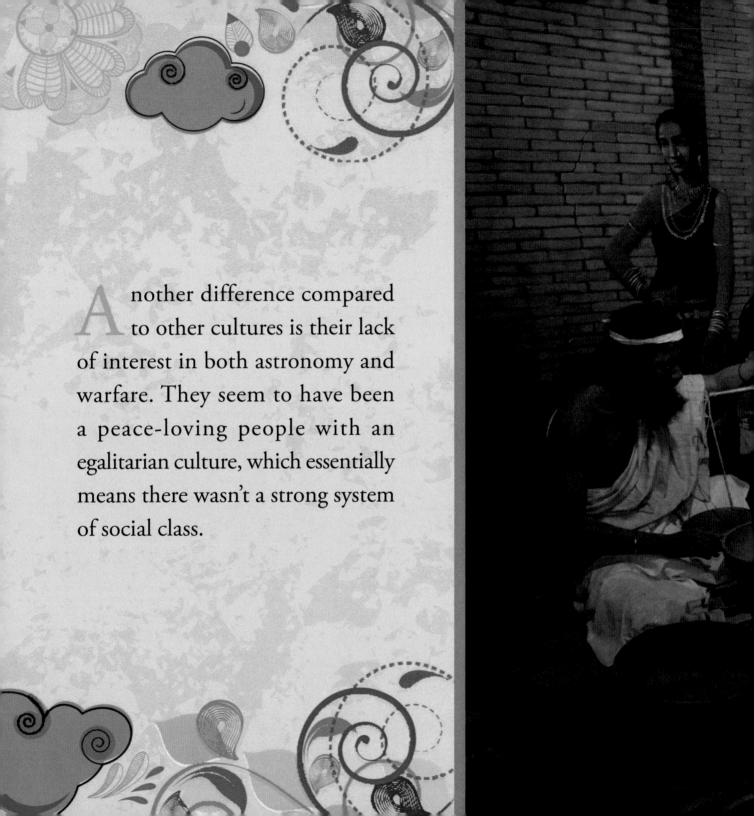

Another difference compared to other cultures is their lack of interest in both astronomy and warfare. They seem to have been a peace-loving people with an egalitarian culture, which essentially means there wasn't a strong system of social class.

INDUS VALLEY CIVILIZATION

INDUS VALLEY RUINS

Circa 1500 BCE, the earliest civilization in the Indus Valley declined. No one knows the exact reason. It could have been an enormous earthquake or other natural disaster, such as a severe change in the climate. Another possibility is that hostile invaders took over the culture.

WELL AT INDUS VALLEY CIVILIZATION SITE, PUPNAGAR, PUNJAB

THE VEDIC PERIOD

About 1500 BCE, tribes of Indo-European peoples, also described as Aryans, began coming to the Indus Valley. They were originally from the area around the Black Sea as well as the area around the Caspian Sea. They spread out in all directions.

A HINDU PAINTING

HITTITES

Some traveled to the continent of Europe, where their culture influenced the ancient Romans and Greeks. Some settled in what is now modern-day Turkey, where they were called Hittites. Some journeyed to Iran, but others journeyed southeast to modern-day Pakistan and onward to the lands of modern-day India.

The Indo-European Influence

Not all historians agree about the path of the Aryans, however, their spoken language, which was written in Sanskrit, has roots that are very similar to Greek as well as Latin, both languages with Indo-European influence.

A great deal of the vocabulary is common among the languages they brought to these widespread locations. Today, there is a great deal of work being done to track DNA throughout history, and some of this research points to the migration of the Aryans into the Indus Valley as well.

The Vedas

The Aryans either brought their religion to India or adapted some of the beliefs of Hinduism that already existed in the Indus Valley. The Vedas, the songs and stories that make up the most ancient of the Hindu scriptures, were first recorded in Sanskrit.

HAYAGRIVA RESTORING VEDAS
TO BRAHMA WHICH WERE
TAKEN TO RASATALA

This language was originally a language that was spoken, not written. Later, it was written using various writing systems including Devanagari, which was the beginning of the language of Hindi—the core language in the country of India today.

ARYANS SETTLING IN INDIA

The Aryans also brought horses that had been domesticated. It's believed that the Aryans were still somewhat nomadic when they arrived at the Indus Valley.

The Caste System

The Aryans established their civilization in the same locations in the Indus Valley where the earlier peoples had lived. They began to intermix and intermarry with the local indigenous people.

PHOTOS FROM SEVENTY-TWO SPECIMENS OF CASTES IN INDIA

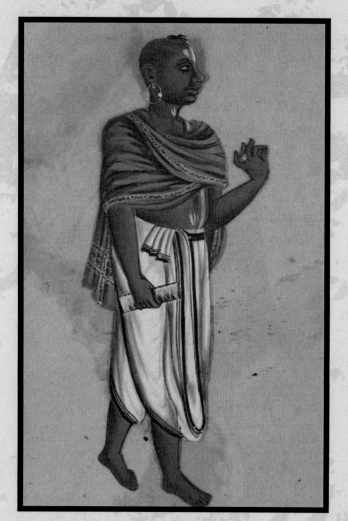

Historians believe that this is when the complicated caste system got started in India. No one knows exactly how it began, but it was the opposite of the egalitarian type of society that had existed in the Indus Valley before.

A caste system is basically a system where people are grouped at different levels in society. These levels are considered permanent and those who were at a certain level gave that same level to their children. There were also smaller specific groups within each caste.

Here are the castes that existed from the highest level of society down to the lowest:

Brahmins

These were the priests. They were considered pure and were at the top level of society.

BARDAI BRAHMINS

Kshatriyas

These were the leaders and warriors. They were considered almost as high level as the Brahmins.

KSHATRIYA KULAVANTAS

Vaisyas

These were the merchants and craftspeople. Skilled workers and landowners were also placed in this category.

Sudra

These were the workers who worked on farms or who were servants. This was the lowest level in the caste system. This was the largest group of people. They didn't own land, but instead worked for the Vaisyas.

Dalits (Untouchables)

This group was even lower than all the castes. The Dalits did all the worst jobs, such as removing dead bodies and cleaning feces out of the street. The Dalits were seen as "polluted" and "dirty."

WANDERING OF ARYAN TRIBES

When the Aryans arrived, they relegated the native peoples to the Dalits group. People were not supposed to marry someone or associate with someone who was from a different caste. Today, this system has been made unconstitutional, but unfortunately in some rural areas there is still prejudice based on the caste system.

The culture of the Aryans and native people of the Indus Valley expanded and different kingdoms began as the centuries went on.

SUMMARY

The Indus Valley civilization, which began in 3200 BCE, was the most populated of the four early civilizations on Earth. For hundreds of years, the people of the Indus Valley lived as equals in relative peace and harmony. Trade was important to them and there is evidence that they traded with Mesopotamia. Then, around 1500 BCE, the Aryans arrived and a strict caste system was introduced. Despite the inequalities in society, the culture flourished and expanded throughout the land of what is now modern-day India.

ARCHAEOLOGICAL RUINS AT MOHENJO DARO

Now that you've read about the history of ancient India, you may want to read about the history of ancient China in the Baby Professor book, Ancient China for Kids - Early Dynasties, Civilization and History | Ancient History for Kids | 6th Grade Social Studies.

Visit

BABY PROFESSOR
EDUCATION KIDS

www.BabyProfessorBooks.com

to download Free Baby Professor eBooks
and view our catalog of new and exciting
Children's Books

Made in the USA
Las Vegas, NV
13 July 2024